# OVERCOME YOUR ANXIETY

DAILY PRACTICE
AND BREATHWORK
FOR A CALMER,
PANIC-FREE LIFE

Susan Reynolds

**chartwell
books**

# Quarto

This edition published in 2024 by Chartwell Books,
an imprint of The Quarto Group
142 West 36th Street, 4th Floor
New York, NY 10018 USA
T (212) 779-4972 F (212) 779-6058
www.Quarto.com

10 9 8 7 6 5 4 3 2 1

Chartwell titles are also available at discount for retail, wholesale, promotional,
and bulk purchase. For details, contact the Special Sales Manager by email at
specialsales@quarto.com or by mail at The Quarto Group, Attn: Special Sales
Manager, 100 Cummings Center Suite 265D, Beverly, MA 01915, USA.

ISBN: 978-0-7858-4403-7

Publisher: Wendy Friedman
Senior Publishing Manager: Meredith Mennitt
Senior Design Manager: Michael Caputo
Editor: Joanne O'Sullivan
Designer: Kate Sinclair

All stock design elements ©Shutterstock

Printed in China

# CONTENTS

# WHAT IS ANXIETY?

## ANXIETY IS A NORMAL HUMAN RESPONSE TO PERCEIVED DANGER.

Thanks to thousands of years of hardwiring, the parasympathetic (nervous) system is always on guard. If it senses something that could potentially harm us, the resultant anxiety alerts our brains to possible danger. Once alarmed, our bodies respond by releasing adrenaline, heightening our senses, increasing our heart rate, and preparing us to fight or flee (or occasionally freeze).

Unfortunately, elevated states of anxiety often happen in response to common stressors—fearing competitive events, feeling overwhelmed, fighting with loved ones, or facing an uncertain future. In our fast-paced, ever-changing, highly fragmented, and perilous lives, elevated states of anxiety have become extremely common.

In fact, approximately one in four Americans regularly suffers elevated levels of anxiety, affecting choices about how they spend their time, what they invest their energy in, and who they allow into their inner circle. When unduly anxious, these choices are based on attempts to avoid fear and vulnerability rather than by heartfelt, genuine desires to live full, meaningful, active lives. Enduring elevated levels of anxiety keeps us in real danger of allowing it to limit our lives.

> *This book will focus on making common, elevated states of anxiety more manageable. We'll offer proven techniques for tamping down anxiety and living your life from a place of centered calm.*

" ANXIETY IS THE
APPREHENSION,
CUED OFF BY A
THREAT TO SOME VALUE
THAT THE INDIVIDUAL
HOLDS ESSENTIAL, TO
HIS EXISTENCE AS A
PERSONALITY. "

—ROLLO MAY

*THE MEANING OF ANXIETY*

# WHAT IS CLINICAL ANXIETY?

Clinical anxiety is a psychological illness that needs medical intervention. Anxiety becomes clinical when elevated anxiety happens far too often, for far too long, becoming so chronic it hampers your daily life; it also occurs at a higher level of intensity. The Diagnostic and Statistical Manual of Mental Disorders, Fifth Edition (DSM-5) defines clinical anxiety disorder as...

*ongoing anxiety or apprehensive expectation (worrying) about events or activities in which you experience three, or more, of the following symptoms, occurring more days than not in for at least six months, including:*

1   *Restlessness, feeling keyed up or on edge, or regularly feeling fatigued*

2   *Difficulty concentrating, your mind going blank, or irritability*

3   *Muscle tension*

4   *Sleep disturbances*

5   *Intrusive or unwelcome thoughts*

# WHEN IS IT CLINICAL ANXIETY?

Clinical anxiety disorders differ from "normal" anxiety in their intensity, duration, their ongoing nature, and their evolution to identifiable phobias. Clinical anxiety disorders include:

Panic disorders that happen more than once a month and are accompanied by irrational fears

Agoraphobia (fear of leaving your house), social phobia, or other specific phobias that cause evasive panic attacks

Generalized anxiety disorder, or chronic anxiety that lasts more than six months and causes muscle tension or rapid heartbeats

Obsessive compulsive (OCD), recurring obsessions or compulsions to perform rituals designed to relieve anxiety

Post-traumatic stress disorder (PTSD), flashbacks, emotional numbing, and anxiety that occurs after experiencing a traumatic event.

*Note: If you are experiencing any of the above, please discuss your ongoing anxiety symptoms with your doctor. Clinical anxiety requires professional help.*

# HOW DOES ANXIETY DIFFER FROM FIGHT OR FLIGHT RESPONSE?

When your brain senses a threat, your sympathetic nervous system responds by:

Moving blood away from your digestive system and other nonvital organs

Boosting glucose production

Releasing adrenaline

Tamping down short and long-term memory

Increasing heart rate and blood pressure.

These deeply ingrained, automatic responses were hardwired into humans when predators were around every bush, and our ancient ancestors had to respond quickly. Even though we presently don't often face threats from wild animals, our brains will still respond to a perceived threat with the flight or fight response. When your body is "locked" in flight or fight mode, it's hard for your brain to figure out if the threat is genuine or if it stems from an unconscious biological response to past traumas. Thus, learning how to calm and quiet your nervous system allows opportunities to then address the underlying cause of your current anxiety.

The problem arises when there is no threat causing this reaction and yet you repeatedly respond *as if* there were. Chronic fearful responses to non-threatening situations take a toll on your nervous system.

# WHAT CAUSES ANXIETY?

Most of our anxiety comes from past experiences or from what we've witnessed or learned from those around us, so anything that traumatized us, or those closest to us, may trigger fearful responses. And, simply put, we live in anxious times; which means our anxiety could also be due to a combination of concerns over:

- Career, future possibilities, personal finances, or economic conditions, instability

- The stress, competitive atmosphere, and insecurity of high-pressure jobs

- Excessive responsibilities or high expectations

- Health challenges

- Family and social relationships

- Climate change

- Divisive politics.

*Since these experiences and pressures are unavoidable, learning to manage anxiety is an essential skill.*

# WHY IT'S IMPORTANT TO MANAGE ANXIETY

Uncontrolled, chronic anxiety not only limits what you do or don't do in your life, it takes a serious toll on your physical and emotional health. If you don't learn how to manage occasional anxiety, chronic symptoms can lead to serious physical health problems, such as ulcers, and psychological problems, such as phobias. Anxious people become fearful people, who then create self-imposed limitations on their lives.

Now that you know the basics, let's discuss *your* anxiety and how it manifests.

"Anxiety is a thin stream of fear trickling through the mind. If encouraged, it cuts a channel into which all other thoughts are drained."

Arthur Somers Roche

" ANXIETY ALARMS
ARE REAL. WHEN
YOUR THOUGHTS SPIN
OUT OF CONTROL AND
YOUR BODY BEGINS
TO BETRAY YOU, IT'S
TERRIFYING. "

—DR. JOHN DELONY,

*REDEFINING ANXIETY:*
*WHAT IT IS, WHAT IT ISN'T,*
*AND HOW TO GET YOUR LIFE BACK*

# HOW DOES *YOUR* ANXIETY MANIFEST?

Each person's degree of and experience with anxiety is unique. Fear and anxiety are experienced in various ways—cognitive, emotional, imaginal, physical, and behavioral.

> Cognitively...

when you are obsessively worrying, you're imagining what "might happen" in the future. When you're obsessively ruminating, you're fruitlessly replaying what happened in the past. Anxiety can be the result of your mind thinking you are in danger, or your tendency to be so self-critical it feels debilitating.

> Emotionally...

you may misinterpret other emotions as anxiety. For example, your underlying emotion might be anger, sadness, surprise, disgust, or even shame, but it feels like anxiety because anxiety may be easier for you to recognize and express.

> Behaviorally...

you may have developed repetitive actions to quell anxiety, like biting your fingernails, tapping your foot, or pulling your hair. You may also use avoidance as your primary coping method, or rely on "bad habits," such as overeating or drinking to distract yourself. Or you may create an argument or become aggressive.

symptoms reflective of anxiety include:

• Shortness of breath or shallow, rapid breathing
• Racing heart or palpitations
• Dizziness, lightheadedness, sweating, blushing, dry mouth
• Nervousness, upset stomach, trembling, or feeling "shaky"
• Tensing your muscles, headaches
• Restlessness, irritability, or fatigue
• Intrusive thoughts that cannot be easily dismissed.

Imaginatively...

when your anxiety results from what your mind creates. Often, they are thoughts not based in reality, or repetitious thoughts and feelings from something that happened in your past.

"Ours is not the task of fixing the entire world all at once, but of stretching out to mend the part of the world that is within our reach."

Clarissa Pinkola Estés

# WHAT MAKES
# YOU ANXIOUS?

Identifying what makes you feel anxious is the first step in learning to overcome it. Because being specific and narrowing your focus will help you throughout this process, give some thought before answering the following questions:

What are your primary stressors? Make a list of what typically creates anxiety in your life.

HOW DOES YOUR ANXIETY MANIFEST?

How manageable are these stressors? Are you proactive in addressing them? If not, why?

What kinds of situations make you feel anxious?

Are there specific activities you avoid due to anxiety? List any activities you avoid.

Are there people you avoid due to anxiety? Write down their names and why you feel anxious around them.

_____
_____
_____
_____
_____
_____
_____
_____
_____
_____
_____
_____
_____
_____
_____
_____
_____
_____
_____
_____
_____
_____

What do you worry about the most? List at least three things that you tend to negatively obsess over.

What do you tend to avoid in fear of feeling anxious? This could be as broad as love or as specific as sexual intimacy.

What social or work situations tend to make you nervous? Identify them and state why they make you feel anxious.

Do you suffer from past traumas or humiliating experiences? What were they? What makes similar thoughts or feelings pop up again? Do you have any triggers?

Do you suffer from self-doubt or personality challenges?

What are *your* physical symptoms?

....................................................................................................................

....................................................................................................................

....................................................................................................................

....................................................................................................................

....................................................................................................................

....................................................................................................................

....................................................................................................................

....................................................................................................................

....................................................................................................................

....................................................................................................................

....................................................................................................................

....................................................................................................................

Using the list of physical symptoms you created, answer the following questions:

Think of the last time you felt anxious and describe what caused it and how your body responded.

....................................................................................................................

....................................................................................................................

....................................................................................................................

....................................................................................................................

....................................................................................................................

....................................................................................................................

....................................................................................................................

....................................................................................................................

....................................................................................................................

Are there certain situations that always make you feel anxious? What calms you in those circumstances?

Is there something or someone in your life that causes chronic anxiety? Can you pinpoint what elicits that fear?

What needs to change for you to feel less anxious?

# YOUR BEHAVIORAL SYMPTOMS

Noticing what you do while feeling anxious can help both in identifying causes and in treating your conditioned response. Examples of anxious behavior includes:

- Avoiding situations and activities associated with anxiety, or fleeing a place when you feel anxious

- Gripping armrests, chairs, steering wheel, etcetera

- Holding your breath or hyperventilating

- Staying near people who help you feel safe

- Always needing "safety objects" (e.g., water bottles, sanitizer)

- Calling friends to distract yourself from anxious feelings

- Having ritualistic behaviors that help you feel safe

- Avoiding eye contact

- Biting fingernails, picking skin, pulling hair

- Avoiding anxiety-provoking topics or activities

- Self-medicating with alcoholic beverages and/or illegal drugs

- Tensing certain muscles

Now, let's take a look at how you behave when anxious.

When I feel anxious, I...

........................................................................................

........................................................................................

........................................................................................

What I need in that moment is...

........................................................................................

........................................................................................

........................................................................................

The thing I obsess most about is...

........................................................................................

........................................................................................

........................................................................................

The best way for me to stop obsessing is to...

........................................................................................

........................................................................................

........................................................................................

If there's something I'm afraid to do, I...

........................................................................................

........................................................................................

........................................................................................

Anxiety drives me to...

........................................................................................

........................................................................................

........................................................................................

# COMMON BEHAVIORAL SYMPTOMS OF ANXIETY

Certain behaviors reflect chronic, elevated anxiety. Fearfulness, excessive worrying, avoidance, isolation, and lethargy are all undesirable emotional states that need to be addressed. According to Dr. Peg O'Connor, professor of philosophy at Gustavus Adolphus College, anxiety becomes a problem when:

You have trouble prioritizing. Everything you need to do feels equal. Cleaning out your closet feels equal to finishing a work project though only one carries the possibility of consequences. Soon, you feel so overwhelmed you fall behind on what must be done.

You procrastinate. You create long, meticulous "to-do" lists, but somehow accomplish little.

You get caught up in *if onlys* and *what ifs*. You focus on imagining consequences—that may or may not happen—or put too many conditions on doing even the simplest things.

You doubt your own decision-making process. Soon you are ignoring your instincts and not making any decisions.

You become perfectionistic. Anything less than perfection feels like abject failure. Even a minor mistake confirms your shortcomings or unworthiness.

You assume everything will be a disaster. If you link "bad" with less than perfect, it becomes hard to imagine that anything good will happen.

You try to control everything. You think controlling all aspects will help you manage your worry and dread.

Have you noticed yourself responding in any of the ways mentioned on the previous page? Which ones cause you the most distress?

........................................................................................................................

........................................................................................................................

........................................................................................................................

........................................................................................................................

........................................................................................................................

........................................................................................................................

........................................................................................................................

........................................................................................................................

........................................................................................................................

........................................................................................................................

........................................................................................................................

........................................................................................................................

........................................................................................................................

........................................................................................................................

........................................................................................................................

........................................................................................................................

........................................................................................................................

........................................................................................................................

........................................................................................................................

........................................................................................................................

........................................................................................................................

Go over your list of anxiety-provoking events and highlight the ones that most often manifest. How does each event manifest?

How can you address each one?

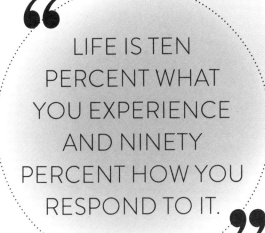

**"LIFE IS TEN PERCENT WHAT YOU EXPERIENCE AND NINETY PERCENT HOW YOU RESPOND TO IT."**

—DOROTHY M. NEDDERMEYER

# WHEN TO SEEK PROFESSIONAL HELP

While we all feel anxious from time to time, warning signs you need professional help include:

- Excessive anxiety that regularly interferes with your everyday life

- Misusing drugs or alcohol to deal with stress or anxiety

- Experiencing irrational fears or feeling out of control

- A significant change in your sleeping, eating, or personal hygiene habits

- A prolonged low mood or depression

- Self-harming, thinking about self-harming, or suicidal thoughts.

*If you suffer from any of these symptoms, please consult a doctor.*

How do *you* react when anxious? Reactivity is what we do without thinking or later reflecting on our behavior. It's always helpful to subjectively view your own behavior and alter it when necessary.

When you feel anxious, do you cancel plans? How often? Which activities or events do you typically dread?

When you feel anxious, do you strike defensive postures? What does that look like?

When you feel anxious, do you isolate yourself until it passes? What other behaviors do you employ to stave off anxiety?

What would it take to address the cause of your anxiety head-on?

# FEAR VERSUS ANXIETY

According to Dr. Sarah Orsillo and Dr. Lizbeth Roemer, authors of *The Mindful Way through Anxiety*, fear and anxiety can feel similar, but have distinct differences. When faced with a threat, we feel a surge of fear until the threat subsides and we feel safe. Conversely, an anxious response will linger until we've come up with a solution; which creates a feeling of restlessness and irritability.

|  | Fear | Anxiety |
| --- | --- | --- |
| **Nature of the threat** | Immediate and real | Future possibilities |
| **Physical response** | Surge of panic | Chronic tension and anxiety |
| **Function** | Survival | Preparedness |

...........................................................................................................

"I can be changed by what happens to me. But I refuse to be reduced by it."

...........................................................................................................

Maya Angelou, *Letter to My Daughter*

# EMBRACE YOUR ANXIETY

Denying or suppressing anxiety can intensify it. To claim your anxiety, ask yourself the following questions:

If anxiety brings insights, what has your anxiety revealed about you?

........................................................................................................

........................................................................................................

........................................................................................................

........................................................................................................

........................................................................................................

........................................................................................................

........................................................................................................

........................................................................................................

........................................................................................................

........................................................................................................

........................................................................................................

........................................................................................................

........................................................................................................

........................................................................................................

........................................................................................................

........................................................................................................

........................................................................................................

........................................................................................................

........................................................................................................

........................................................................................................

What are some factors that create or intensify your anxiety?

What strategies can you use to shift a fearful mindset to one that welcomes anxiety?

How can your anxiety help you learn more about yourself and grow?

What one thing will you try tomorrow to flip from denying to recognizing and accepting anxiety?

> "THE LARGEST PART OF WHAT WE CALL 'PERSONALITY' IS DETERMINED BY HOW WE'VE OPTED TO DEFEND OURSELVES AGAINST ANXIETY AND SADNESS."

—ALAIN DE BOTTON

# DON'T GET OVER IT

Amy Scher, author of *How to Heal Yourself from Anxiety*, says anyone who chides you to "just get over it," is wrong. Here are three reasons she says dealing with anxiety is the only way through:

( 1 ) **YOUR BODY IS IN FREAK-OUT MODE.** *When it feels threatened, your brain automatically responds with "flight or fight" chemicals. This happens whether you want it to, not, and it's your body's primary defense system, which is why you want it to keep responding appropriately.*

( 2 ) **EMOTIONS ARE LODGED IN YOUR BODY.** *Whether it's triggered emotions from past trauma, or new emotions generated by what's happening, you need to identify and feel your emotions, and not deny or repress them.*

( 3 ) **YOUR ANXIETY MAY BE SERVING A PURPOSE.** *Your subconscious mind may create anxiety as a form of protection. Before dismissing the uncomfortable feelings, it's helpful to figure out why your subconscious feels you need protection.*

According to Scher, rather than "getting over" anxiety, it's important to examine the underlying causes and work through whatever is needed to disengage from automatic responses.

Now that you've identified and explored how your anxiety manifests, let's move on to proven techniques that will help you overcome your anxiety.

" FEAR AND ANXIETY MANY TIMES INDICATES THAT WE ARE MOVING IN A POSITIVE DIRECTION, OUT OF THE SAFE CONFINES OF OUR COMFORT ZONE, AND IN THE DIRECTION OF OUR TRUE PURPOSE. "

—CHARLES F. GLASSMAN

*BRAIN DRAIN:*
*THE BREAKTHROUGH THAT*
*WILL CHANGE YOUR LIFE*

# TRY GENERAL RELAXATION TECHNIQUES

When anxiety strikes, certain techniques can help you tamp down anxious feelings and ramp up calm. Since rapid breathing is one of the primary responses to anxiety, the first line of defense is to slow your breathing.

## USE BREATHING TO CALM ANXIETY

Most anxiety is exacerbated by rapid breathing. Therefore, slowing down your breathing is the ideal first step. Here are three ways you can slow down your breathing.

> Try Calming Breaths

Breathing slowly decreases rapid breaths and calms frayed nerves. To calm anxiety, breathe in slowly to the count of ten then breathe out slowly to the count of ten. Keep your focus solely on your breathing, how it feels to draw air in, and how it feels as you exhale.

> Practice Abdominal Diaphragmatic Breathing

Breathing from your abdomen helps you ground yourself in the present moment and slow down automatic physical reactions. As you draw in a breath through your nose, focus on drawing it down through your lungs and deep into your belly, hold it for two or three seconds, then slowly release. Purse your lips as if preparing for a kiss and imagine that you are using your stomach muscles to push the air out. Place a hand on your belly to bring your focus there and monitor how it rises and falls with each deep breath and release.

## Try Counting Breaths

Forcing yourself to count each breath you take (slow breaths, please!) helps you tamp down anxious thoughts and refocus your body and your mind. Breathe slowly in and out, counting each breath. If you lose count, just start over. Keep breathing and counting until the anxiety subsides.

## Switch Nostrils

Press your right nostril closed and breathe in deeply through your left nostril. Release the breath slowly, then lift your finger, press your left nostril closed, and breathe in deeply before breathing out slowly. Keep repeating until you feel calm.

## Try Sighing

If your breaths are shallow, try a deep sigh. Studies have shown that cyclic sighing, in which your exhale lasts longer than your inhale, can effectively improve your mood. Audibly sighing can also be a quick way to reset your breathing and gain better control.

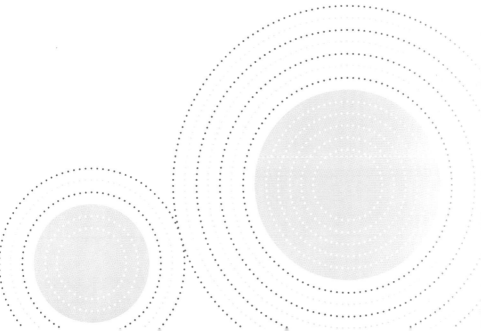

# PRACTICE DAILY FOR TWO WEEKS

According to the authors of *Coping with Anxiety*, practicing abdominal breathing and calming breaths twice a day, for five to ten minutes each session, can help those forms of breathing become habitual, and therefore automatic, when anxiety strikes. Over time, this regular practice will help you reverse the physiological reactions of panic and anxiety.

Keep a log of your breathing practice. Were you able to follow a schedule? What have you observed?

........................................................................................................................

........................................................................................................................

........................................................................................................................

........................................................................................................................

........................................................................................................................

........................................................................................................................

........................................................................................................................

........................................................................................................................

........................................................................................................................

........................................................................................................................

........................................................................................................................

........................................................................................................................

........................................................................................................................

........................................................................................................................

........................................................................................................................

........................................................................................................................

........................................................................................................................

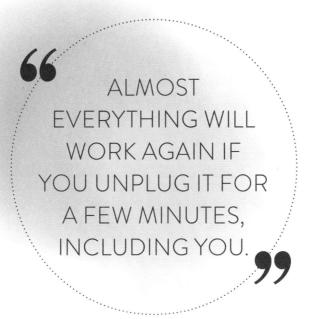

**"ALMOST EVERYTHING WILL WORK AGAIN IF YOU UNPLUG IT FOR A FEW MINUTES, INCLUDING YOU."**

—ANNE LAMOTT

# USE GROUNDING EXERCISES TO DISRUPT ANXIETY

According to Dr. Mary Catherine McDonald, author of *Unbroken: The Trauma Response Is Never Wrong*, these are some of the most effective ways to deflect burgeoning anxiety.

> Scan your body.

Sit with both feet solidly on the ground. If it feels even more reassuring, tuck your hands under your thighs. Talking aloud, describe how it feels to have your feet solidly on the ground. Are they meeting a soft carpet or a cold, hard floor? Move your focus up your legs and describe how they feel against the chair. Next, notice how your back feels against the chair. Do you feel fully supported? Keep scanning your body until you feel your muscles relax.

> Stop and look.

Stop thinking and focus on noticing what's in the room. What colors do you see? Who's around you? What are people wearing? What are you hearing? Is it cold or warm? What can you smell? Keep doing this until your anxiety subsides.

## Move mindfully.

Stop what you are doing and take a walk. Notice how your feet feel meeting the ground. Notice how your body feels when your weight shifts from one leg to the other. Notice how easy or tight your gait becomes. If you have trouble focusing, simply count your steps, ten at a time, until your brain calms itself.

## Visualize yourself in a safe place.

Your brain can imaginatively transport you to another place. Simply pause, focus on slow breaths, and visualize a safe or happy place. Notice specifics about the place and what makes you feel safe or happy, then imagine yourself in that space. What sounds, smells, tastes, feelings come to mind? Feel them!

## Count backwards.

If your brain is racing down the anxiety pathway, one way to put on the brakes is to count backwards. This shakes up your frontal cortex, where most of the anxious thinking is happening.

## Ice it out.

If your anxiety is spiraling out of control, splashing your face with cold water, running cold water over your hands and wrists, or even holding an ice cube to your inner wrist will deflect an anxious brain and give you time to consciously address your anxiety.

# GO ZEN

One simple way to distract an anxious brain is to buy yourself a Tibetan sound bowl. Then, when anxiety becomes problematic, you could subvert obsessive thoughts or uncontrollable emotions by focusing on running your fingers around the bowl's rim and attuning yourself to the sensation of that action—as well as the vibration it creates.

"All negativity is caused by an accumulation of psychological time and denial of the present. Unease, anxiety, tension, stress, worry–all forms of fear–are caused by too much future, and not enough presence."

Eckhart Tolle, *The Power of Now: A Guide to Spiritual Enlightenment*

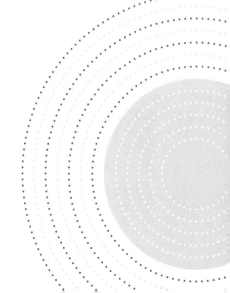

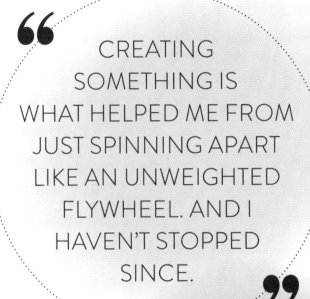

"CREATING SOMETHING IS WHAT HELPED ME FROM JUST SPINNING APART LIKE AN UNWEIGHTED FLYWHEEL. AND I HAVEN'T STOPPED SINCE."

—STEPHEN COLBERT

# GIVE YOURSELF A TASK

Distracting an anxious brain can be as simple as giving it something else to do. If you're in a situation that makes you feel anxious, sit down with your phone, or pen and paper, and quickly make a list of what you can and what you cannot control in this anxiety-producing situation. Typically, you can control your own behavior and response, such as removing yourself from the situation, and you cannot control others' behavior—though you can set boundaries. Just seeing what's possible and being proactive will help you overcome your anxiety.

## EMPLOY REALITY TESTING

When you feel anxious, particularly if you're someone who tends to overreact, it's essential you pause to determine whether there's a genuine threat or you're perceiving danger based purely on thoughts or feelings— has something from your past triggered anxiety in the current moment? Are you projecting into the future?

The second part would be to assess whether you have any control over what happens, then decide what you can do *in that particular situation* to reduce your anxiety. In most instances, the only real thing we have control over is how we respond. Gaining mastery over your anxiety gives you more opportunities to consciously choose how you respond.

Think about the last time you felt anxious. Was there a genuine threat? If not, what triggered your anxiety?

Do you typically overreact? List five times you jumped to the wrong conclusion and suffered unnecessary anxiety.

" SOMETIMES THE MOST IMPORTANT THING IN A WHOLE DAY IS THE REST WE TAKE BETWEEN TWO DEEP BREATHS. "

—ETTY HILLESUM

# CREATE A
# VISUAL REMINDER

It helps to create a visual chart reflecting what you can and cannot control. Try drawing a circle on a large piece of paper. Inside the circle, write down what you can control (e.g., your thoughts, attitude, boundaries, words, and actions). Outside the circle, write things you cannot control (e.g., time, what happens around you, whether other people like you, and what other people think, feel, or do). When anxious, take a look at this visual reminder of what you can control and what you need to release.

"The man of courage is not the man who did not face adversity. The man of courage is the man who faced adversity and spoke to it. The man of courage tells adversity, 'You're trespassing, and I give you no authority to steal my joy, my faith or my hope.'"

Kiese Laymon, *How to Slowly Kill Yourself and Others in America*

Use this page for your drawing.

# USE A SOOTHING AFFIRMATION

Spend five minutes repeating a phrase that helps you feel calm:

*"Everything and everyone around me is here to offer support."*

*"I am grounded and safe in my surroundings."*

*"My current feelings will subside, and I will walk gracefully through life."*

It's helpful to write the affirmation that most helps you on a note card and put it somewhere you can see it daily.

It's also helpful to have simple affirmative statements you can repeat when anxious. Saying the affirmations, aloud or silently, will calm anxiety in the moment. If your mind wanders, bring it back to the affirmation and keep repeating it until you feel calm. Examples of these types of simple affirmations would be: "I feel peaceful and calm." "I release my fears and worries." "I am relaxed and free of worry."

Write three detailed affirmations you could use to instill a sense of safety each day.

1 ................................................................................................................

2 ................................................................................................................

3 ................................................................................................................

Write three simple affirmations you could use when anxiety runs high and you need to calm yourself.

1 ................................................................................................................

2 ................................................................................................................

3 ................................................................................................................

# EXPAND WHO YOU ARE

According to McDonald, creating lists of what your mind is telling you is truly wrong with you, contemplating how lousy that list of negative labels makes you feel, then writing a list of 100 (yes, 100!) things that make you *you*, can help calm anxiety. The point is to move beyond labels and realize that you—like everyone—are complex and not so narrowly defined by your self-created, negative labels. Use this space for your list.

# ENTERTAIN YOURSELF

Watch a movie you've been longing to see (try a comedy to lighten your mood!). Work on a jigsaw puzzle. Clean out your closet. Read a book. Anything that requires your brain to focus on something other than what's making you anxious will work.

List five activities you could do to distract yourself.

1

2

3

4

5

# DO SOMETHING PLEASURABLE

It's hard to be anxious and have fun at the same time. If there's an activity that always brings pleasure, stop fretting and go do it—now!

List five super fun activities you could do when anxious.

1 ................................................................................................

................................................................................................

2 ................................................................................................

................................................................................................

3 ................................................................................................

................................................................................................

4 ................................................................................................

................................................................................................

5 ................................................................................................

................................................................................................

# LISTEN TO MUSIC

Many studies have shown that listening to music can generate an overall decrease in self-reported anxiety. It's recommended that you start by listening to something matching your mood before shifting step by step to more soothing music. As you accustom your brain to the music, you soon begin mentally and physically following along. While the initial music should reflect whatever anxiety you're feeling, the more soothing music you graduate toward should provide release and guide you to a more relaxed place.

Do you have "freak out" or "fight" songs you listen to when anxious, angry, or upset? List five options and the mood they reflect.

1 

2 

3 

4 

5

List five albums or songs you love that create a sense of joy or peace.
Order them so the most calming is listed last.


1
........................................................................................................................
........................................................................................................................
........................................................................................................................

2
........................................................................................................................
........................................................................................................................
........................................................................................................................

3
........................................................................................................................
........................................................................................................................
........................................................................................................................

4
........................................................................................................................
........................................................................................................................
........................................................................................................................

5
........................................................................................................................
........................................................................................................................
........................................................................................................................

List five songs that would induce a meditative state. Nature sounds or even lullabies may do the trick. Hint: Listen nightly to your favorite to transition into sleep.

1
................................................................

2
................................................................

3
................................................................

4
................................................................

5
................................................................

................................................................

Make yourself an "anxiety playlist" that you can call up whenever needed.

................................................................
................................................................
................................................................
................................................................
................................................................
................................................................
................................................................
................................................................
................................................................
................................................................
................................................................

GENERAL RELAXATION TECHNIQUES

# SING IT OUT

To snap out of anxiety, simply singing a song, or humming, stimulates your vagus nerve and thereby calms your nervous system. It doesn't matter what you sing, or how loudly you sing, only that you use the process of singing, or humming, to refocus your anxious brain.

"Music is the language of the spirit. It opens the secret of life bringing peace, abolishing strife."

Kahlil Gibran

Now that we've covered stopgap measures to overcome anxiety in the moment, let's discuss techniques you can use to deepen your ability to manage ongoing anxiety.

# TRY DEFUSION TECHNIQUES TO REDIRECT THINKING

Defusion techniques are designed to disrupt your stream of thoughts and create enough space between your conditioned, automatic thoughts and your awareness of those thoughts, affording you the opportunity to assess what's happening and then consciously choose how to respond. The theory is that, over time, you "fuse" with your thoughts and thereby come to accept them as true. This manifests in three ways:

**1** YOU LINK A THOUGHT TO AN OUTCOME:
*When my heart races, it will lead to a heart attack.*

**2** YOU ADHERE TO STRICT RULES ABOUT BEHAVIOR:
*I must, I should, or I shouldn't, I could never.*

**3** YOU BELIEVE YOUR INNER CRITIC'S WORST ASSESSMENTS:
*You're worthless, You're hopeless, You always fail,* and so on.

The problem with all these manifestations is you're viewing thoughts or images streaming through your mind as absolute truth when, in fact, they may be unfounded.

# KISS REGRETS GOODBYE

Some studies have shown that writing about a negative experience, like regret, for fifteen minutes a day, for three consecutive days, can effectively defuse its potency. When writing about your negative experience and any regrets you may have as a result, ask yourself: "What lessons can I draw from this experience?" and "How can I apply them to my life going forward?"

List 3 regrets you need to purge through writing about them.

1

2

3

"Letting go gives us freedom, and freedom is the only condition for happiness. If, in our heart, we still cling to anything - anger, anxiety, or possessions - we cannot be free."

Thich Nhat Hanh

# DEFUSE NEGATIVE THOUGHTS

When bombarded by thoughts that may have become consciously or unconsciously fused in your thinking, you can defuse them by pausing and asking yourself:

What is my mind telling me to believe about what's happening?

In this moment, what *specific* thoughts are making me uncomfortable?

Can I stop and simply notice what my mind is saying?

Can I identify and dismiss unfair judgments?

Are these thoughts helpful or self-sabotage?

When anxious, it's helpful to write any thoughts down and make an objective assessment. If you discover your thoughts are not accurately depicting the situation or reflecting the feelings making you anxious, it's helpful to view the thoughts as transient and consciously dismiss them.

# CHANGE THE SCALE AND INTENSITY OF YOUR REACTIONS

We often have little to no control over much of what happens, and what other people think, say, or do. What we can control is how we think, speak, and act. Moderating your emotions, however, requires you to first calm anxious thoughts or feelings. Creating space to make a moderated choice is what managing your anxiety is all about.

What are some strategies you could use to step back from the emotion of a moment?

# HOW DO YOUR NEGATIVE THOUGHT PATTERNS INFLUENCE MOOD AND BEHAVIOR?

Left to its own devices, an anxious brain can become obsessed with thoughts and even create its own drama. Let's explore your thought patterns:

When you feel anxious, what thoughts tend to recur most often? What are these thoughts focused on? Is the genesis: Low self-worth? Fear of embarrassment? Fear of failure? Fear of abandonment?

........................................................................................................................

........................................................................................................................

........................................................................................................................

........................................................................................................................

........................................................................................................................

........................................................................................................................

........................................................................................................................

........................................................................................................................

........................................................................................................................

........................................................................................................................

........................................................................................................................

........................................................................................................................

........................................................................................................................

What do you tend to obsess about? Think about lifelong patterns and what your family or friends would see as your thought obsessions. What's beneath these obsessions?

What are your biggest fears? Literally list them and dig beneath the surface to find the real causes: where and when they generated and why they persist.

........................................................................................................

........................................................................................................

........................................................................................................

........................................................................................................

........................................................................................................

........................................................................................................

........................................................................................................

........................................................................................................

........................................................................................................

........................................................................................................

........................................................................................................

........................................................................................................

........................................................................................................

........................................................................................................

........................................................................................................

........................................................................................................

........................................................................................................

........................................................................................................

........................................................................................................

........................................................................................................

........................................................................................................

What makes you feel inadequate or incompetent? Are your perceptions of yourself accurate, or distorted? Write down five things you're particularly good at doing.

Use this space to acknowledge your fears and worries.

**I'm afraid of...**

...............................................................................

...............................................................................

...............................................................................

...............................................................................

...............................................................................

...............................................................................

**I'm *most* afraid of...**

...............................................................................

...............................................................................

...............................................................................

...............................................................................

...............................................................................

...............................................................................

**I'm constantly worried that...**

...............................................................................

...............................................................................

...............................................................................

...............................................................................

...............................................................................

...............................................................................

...............................................................................

# WALK IT OFF

One simple way to overcome anxiety is to "walk it off." Scientists say a ten-minute walk, particularly outside, not only disrupts nonproductive thinking but boosts the feel-good brain chemical dopamine and your ability to sleep at night. Both will help your brain cope with anxiety.

> **WORRYING IS CARRYING TOMORROW'S LOAD WITH TODAY'S STRENGTH— CARRYING TWO DAYS AT ONCE. IT IS MOVING INTO TOMORROW AHEAD OF TIME. WORRYING DOESN'T EMPTY TOMORROW OF ITS SORROW, IT EMPTIES TODAY OF ITS STRENGTH.**
>
> —CORRIE TEN BOOM

# RECOGNIZE AND ALTER HARMFUL THOUGHT PATTERNS

To mitigate distorted thinking, it's helpful to write your thoughts down so you can pinpoint and strike off the distorted ones. Think back to the last time you felt anxious.

What was happening? What were your specific triggers?

Were your triggers based on the present or something from your past?

Write down any "what if" questions going through your head at the time. Are these questions jumping to the worst or most unlikely outcomes?

Of all the things you imagined, what really happened? Do you frequently create scenarios that are overreactions and unlikely to happen? In which areas of your life does this often happen?

........................................................................................................
........................................................................................................
........................................................................................................
........................................................................................................
........................................................................................................
........................................................................................................
........................................................................................................
........................................................................................................
........................................................................................................
........................................................................................................
........................................................................................................
........................................................................................................
........................................................................................................
........................................................................................................
........................................................................................................
........................................................................................................
........................................................................................................
........................................................................................................
........................................................................................................
........................................................................................................
........................................................................................................
........................................................................................................

What could you do differently the next time you feel anxious in a similar situation?

_____

_____

_____

_____

_____

_____

_____

_____

_____

_____

_____

_____

_____

_____

_____

"You don't have to be a victim of your past anymore. You are not your mistakes, and you are not your struggles."

Nick Vujicic, *Life Without Limits*

# THINK POSITIVELY

Happiness is a state of mind one can consciously choose. Replacing negative thoughts with positive thoughts is a crucial step toward developing the skill required to choose happiness. To overcome your anxiety, replace negative, unproductive thoughts with more positive, constructive thoughts and responses. For example, if you're thinking, "Everyone is going to reject me," try thinking, "I'm a likable person who many will enjoy meeting."

List five nonproductive thoughts that regularly create anxiety.

1

2

3

4

5

List five productive thoughts to counteract those assumptions or projections.

1
_____

2
_____

3
_____

4
_____

5
_____

## ADDRESS IT HEAD-ON

*If you feel threatened, lonely, exhausted, short-fused, unable to curb negative thoughts, or fixated on a person or situation that is causing you pain, calming the intensity is helpful; however, you want to probe under the surface and resolve what keeps setting off your alarm system. Ask yourself, "What is troubling me?" Sit still until the answers you need surface, then use your lovely brain to figure out a way to address whatever has been revealed.*

*Now that you've explored how your anxiety manifests and learned techniques for overcoming it in the moment and over time, let's discuss how you can ward off anxiety in your everyday life.*

# WARD OFF ANXIETY

In addition to proactive techniques for disrupting anxiety, you need techniques that will help you ward off everyday anxiety. Practicing these behaviors on a regular basis will both limit anxiety and help you better cope with it when it happens.

## NURTURE RELATIONSHIPS (AND YOURSELF)

Healthy relationships are crucial to our mental health. Are your relationships causing anxiety? What's the problem? How can you fix it?

How does your anxiety specifically impact your relationships?

What causes the most anxiety in your relationships? Fear of abandonment? Fear of being genuinely seen? Fear of not being truly loved? Fear of feeling smothered? Feeling pressured to behave in a certain way?

What prevents you from asking for what you need to feel safe and secure?
Why is revealing your true self stress inducing?

Do you make limited choices based on worry or avoidance? Identify the people or situations you tend to avoid and why.

Which relationships allow you to be fully present? Which relationships make it hard for you to be fully present? What causes the disparity?

"Don't judge each day by the harvest you reap but by the seeds that you plant."

Robert Louis Stevenson

# RE-EVALUATE
# CAREER GOALS

We live in a fast-paced, almost workaholic society. Your anxiety may stem from the simple fact you're attempting too much, too fast. Assess where you are now by answering the following questions:

Are you miserable in your current job? Are you doing what you really want to do?

.................................................................................................

.................................................................................................

.................................................................................................

.................................................................................................

.................................................................................................

.................................................................................................

.................................................................................................

.................................................................................................

.................................................................................................

.................................................................................................

.................................................................................................

.................................................................................................

.................................................................................................

.................................................................................................

.................................................................................................

.................................................................................................

Is your schedule creating stress? Is the commute too far? If you could make a change, what would it be?

When it comes to your career, where can you realistically be in five years? Ten years?

Do you want to change course? If so, what's holding you back? How would your new path look? What do you need to embark on it?

.......................................................................................................................

.......................................................................................................................

.......................................................................................................................

.......................................................................................................................

.......................................................................................................................

.......................................................................................................................

.......................................................................................................................

.......................................................................................................................

.......................................................................................................................

.......................................................................................................................

.......................................................................................................................

.......................................................................................................................

.......................................................................................................................

.......................................................................................................................

.......................................................................................................................

.......................................................................................................................

"Every time you are tempted to react in the same old way, ask if you want to be a prisoner of the past or a pioneer of the future."

Deepak Chopra

# SET REALISTIC EXPECTATIONS

It's great to have lofty goals and hold yourself to high standards, but sometimes our expectations are so high we constantly feel stressed. Your expectations may need a more realistic assessment. Consider the following:

Are your standards for excellence too high? Who created these standards? Are they malleable?

.................................................................................................

.................................................................................................

.................................................................................................

.................................................................................................

.................................................................................................

.................................................................................................

When is "good enough" okay? What makes the difference?

.................................................................................................

.................................................................................................

.................................................................................................

.................................................................................................

.................................................................................................

.................................................................................................

.................................................................................................

.................................................................................................

.................................................................................................

Is the pace at which you're living life too fast? How can you slow it down? What would you prioritize? What would you jettison?

Do you let others determine how you view or live your life? Who has the power to influence your choices? Why have you given them this power? How would they react if you set boundaries?

When it comes to how you live your life, what would be *your* true ideal?
What do *you* most value?

What would it take to help you focus more on the joys of living and less on how much you can get done?

..................................................................................................................................
..................................................................................................................................
..................................................................................................................................
..................................................................................................................................
..................................................................................................................................
..................................................................................................................................
..................................................................................................................................
..................................................................................................................................
..................................................................................................................................
..................................................................................................................................
..................................................................................................................................
..................................................................................................................................
..................................................................................................................................
..................................................................................................................................
..................................................................................................................................
..................................................................................................................................
..................................................................................................................................
..................................................................................................................................
..................................................................................................................................
..................................................................................................................................
..................................................................................................................................
..................................................................................................................................
..................................................................................................................................

# STAMP OUT WORRYING

Worrying can become an unconscious habit, which means realizing when you're caught up in it and choosing new ways to respond can help you break the habit.

What do you worry about the most?

What causes your obsessive worrying?

Has your worrying been productive? Predictive? Exaggerated? Ridiculous?

_____

_____

_____

_____

_____

_____

_____

_____

_____

_____

_____

_____

_____

_____

_____

_____

_____

_____

## DON'T GO DOWN THE CATASTROPHIZING HIGHWAY

*When something happens do you automatically envision the worst? Catastrophizing takes your brain down the negativity highway, and once you have momentum, it's hard to stop. When something feels threatening, stop and ask yourself if the worst is truly going to happen or if something less threatening is the likely outcome.*

# AVOID PROCRASTINATION

Procrastination creates stress and usually involves fear. If you're afraid of failing, it's hard to motivate yourself, but easy to criticize and berate yourself for procrastinating. One way to overcome anxiety is to confront your procrastination head-on.

What do you hate doing?

What avoidance techniques do you use most often? What are the consequences?

_____

_____

_____

_____

_____

_____

_____

_____

_____

_____

_____

_____

_____

_____

_____

_____

_____

_____

_____

_____

_____

_____

What's the fear behind your procrastination? Is it reality-based?

How can you make it easier to tackle undesirable challenges?

List your current challenges.

Strategize solutions for each of these challenges.

# WRITE IT OUT

Identifying what is causing your anxiety helps tamp it down, but writing about it—including the reasons you feel anxious, how it manifests, what thoughts are behind it, and how you can address it—will alleviate anxiety in the present and the future.

Make a list of what has been causing anxiety lately.

Write a paragraph describing your primary concerns or obstacles and what makes them problematic.

What really upsets or frightens you? What's the major fear behind it? Is it reality-based? If it's connected to past trauma, can you release it?

Can the way you think about fearful challenges be changed? What can *you* do to change the situation?

# PUT IT IN WRITING

Commit, in writing, to direct action. Make it a habit to put your worries on paper, allow your brain to stop fretting and focus, instead, on finding solutions.

To overcome what is causing my anxiety, I promise myself I will:

# TELL SOMEONE YOUR STORY

According to McDonald, anything that triggers memories of a traumatic event can amp up anxiety. She recommends the process of "retelling," in which you share, with someone you trust, the initial traumatic events. Triggering events open "a portal." If you walk through it slowly—sorting out what happened, rendering it into a story with a beginning, middle, and end—it allows you to fill in missing pieces, then file the story away; thereby decreasing its ability to trigger future anxiety.

......................................................

"Your story inspires the world.
You are needed on this planet."

......................................................

Hiral Nagda

Now that you know even more about your anxiety, let's discuss concrete strategies for overcoming it in your daily life.

# ACTIVELY COMBAT STRESS

The way you live your life can amp up or tamp down anxiety. The choices you make about how you structure your time, and which activities you do, will affect your ability to cope and enjoy your life. Let's discuss multiple strategies for de-stressing your life and thereby overcoming your anxiety.

## MAKE TIME FOR DOWNTIME

Stress is obviously cumulative. Some people keep themselves so busy they don't pause to see what's causing anxiety in their lives. You need time to feel what you feel and reflect, and creating space for genuine downtime helps your nervous system power down. Sleep is not counted as downtime. Downtime is stepping away from obligations and making time for something you enjoy—that helps you relax, boosts your spirits, or refreshes you. It could be as simple as one hour spent watching a show you love, reading a novel, riding your bike, focusing on a hobby, talking to a friend, or taking a leisurely walk. Minimum suggestions for creating downtime are one hour a day, one day a week, and one week every three to four months.

.......................................................................

"Sometimes our 'stop-doing' list needs to be bigger than our 'to-do' list."

.......................................................................

Patti Digh, *Four-Word Self-Help: Simple Wisdom for Complex Lives*

Downtime can be as simple as pausing to read for an hour, taking a hot bath, calling a friend, hitting baseballs at the batting cages, listening to music, or sitting in silence. Do you have downtime now? If not, how can you create one hour a day and one day a week for downtime?

List five things you could do with your downtime for one hour, then for one day. Schedule them in your calendar.

1

2

3

4

5

What types of restorative things would you like to do once every three or four months? A spa weekend? A short trip to the mountains? A reading retreat?

List three things you'll schedule for quarterly breaks in the near future.

# COUNT YOUR BLESSINGS

Taking a few minutes each night to acknowledge every person you encountered that day, wish them solace, and thank them for whatever they brought to your day can significantly boost your emotional connection. This kind of loving positivity is a productive habit to form.

Who did you encounter recently who brought joy into your life?

......................................................................................................

......................................................................................................

......................................................................................................

......................................................................................................

*Who* are you particularly thankful for?

......................................................................................................

......................................................................................................

......................................................................................................

......................................................................................................

What happened today that brightened your world?

......................................................................................................

......................................................................................................

......................................................................................................

......................................................................................................

......................................................................................................

......................................................................................................

Feelings inform us about how we're doing in the wider world, but often they are overblown or not to be trusted. If you're dismissive or short with someone out of what feels like frustration, you may seem like a lousy friend or spouse when, in truth, you're simply too tired to be your usual kind, responsive self. Anger can occur when something surprises or disappoints us and we snap in response. However, if we wait to process what's causing the pain, we'd likely choose a different response. Mastering your emotions reduces anxiety because you accept your feelings as signals of what's important—what's bothering you—then *consciously choose* how to respond from a more centered, calm space.

Which emotions are an ongoing struggle for you?

Can you pinpoint what makes your difficult emotions problematic? What typically triggers them? How can you address the sources?

# OVERCOMING ANXIETY GUIDELINES

To overcome anxiety, the Anxiety and Depression Association of America advises you to:

- Accept that you cannot control everything.

- Settle for your best rather than aim for perfection.

- Learn what triggers your stress and anxiety.

- Write about your frustrations in a journal.

- Focus on the positive aspects of your life.

- Enlarge your support group.

- Find outlets for your frustration—try volunteering, for example.

Use this workbook as a resource for techniques to tamp down anxiety. Repeat the exercises until they become rote.

" IN MOMENTS OF PANIC, RIDE THE WAVE, WHICH MEANS ALLOWING YOURSELF TO EXPERIENCE THE ANXIETY AND WAITING UNTIL IT ABATES — WHICH IT WILL. MOST PANIC ATTACKS PEAK AND SUBSIDE IN TEN TO FIFTEEN MINUTES. "

—DR. KEVIN CHAPMAN

As we grow up, many of us lose our ability to play. Play, however, is a fabulous way to reduce stress, tension, and anxiety. Playing games with friends, gathering for an old-fashioned game of charades, going rollerblading, renting a canoe for a day, playing sports, or spending the day at a lake are all ways to add play to your life.

When was the last time you played? What were you doing?

"It is a happy talent to know how to play."

Ralph Waldo Emerson

When was your last vacation? Describe what an ideal vacation would look like. How can you budget to make it—or something close to ideal—happen?

Do you have hobbies that bring you joy? How about going to the movies, playing a sport you enjoy (with friends!), cooking or baking for fun? List any hobbies you'd like to revive or new hobbies to pursue.

Are there any sports or activities you'd love to explore? Classes you'd like to take? As long as you'd consider it fun, it could be on anything. List five ideas for opening yourself up to more playful activities.

.................................................................................................................................

.................................................................................................................................

.................................................................................................................................

.................................................................................................................................

.................................................................................................................................

.................................................................................................................................

.................................................................................................................................

.................................................................................................................................

.................................................................................................................................

.................................................................................................................................

.................................................................................................................................

.................................................................................................................................

.................................................................................................................................

.................................................................................................................................

.................................................................................................................................

.................................................................................................................................

.................................................................................

"If you are losing your leisure, look out!
It may be you are losing your soul."
.................................................................................

Virginia Woolf

How can you make more time for joyful activities? Literally get in the habit of earmarking time for play in your calendar. Start now by committing to two joyful activities you'll schedule in the near future.

" FOR
FAST-ACTING
RELIEF,
TRY SLOWING
DOWN. "

—LILY TOMLIN

# SHARE BURDENS WITH TRUSTED FRIENDS OR FAMILY

Friends and family can be valuable resources for validating reality and offering support. Do you avail yourself of their wise counsel? If not, why?

..............................................................................................................

..............................................................................................................

..............................................................................................................

..............................................................................................................

..............................................................................................................

..............................................................................................................

..............................................................................................................

When was the last time you talked honestly with someone about what frightens you? What was it?

..............................................................................................................

..............................................................................................................

..............................................................................................................

..............................................................................................................

..............................................................................................................

..............................................................................................................

..............................................................................................................

..............................................................................................................

Who did you tell? How did they react?

What, if anything, are you currently hiding? Why? Who could you trust to share it with?

List any fears or concerns you're currently experiencing. Are they based on past traumas? Does the threat still exist?

How would successfully sharing your fears manifest? Note: Writing about a past trauma for fifteen minutes—once a day for three days—helps to dissipate its potency.

# GET READY,
# GET SET, WORRY

Dr. Dave Carbonell, co-author of *The Worry Trick*, recommends you make an appointment with yourself each week to worry. He even suggests you do ten minutes of focused worrying aloud, in front of a mirror so you can see yourself worrying. This helps, he says, in bringing worries to the forefront—instead of them thrumming somewhat unattended in the background—and eventually reducing the amount of worrying you do.

What are you worried about? What typically causes you the most worry? Are these worries reality-based or exaggerated?

" YOU NEED TO UNDERSTAND THE SOURCES OF YOUR ANXIETY OR DEPRESSION, ADDRESS THEM, AND TRAIN YOUR MIND TO BETTER PROCESS SOURCES OF STRESS GOING FORWARD.

THIS RELIEVES PAIN COMING FROM THIS SOURCE IN THE SAME WAY YOUR BONE HEALING RELIEVES THE PAIN FROM A BROKEN ARM. "

—CONGRESSMAN ADAM SMITH

AUTHOR OF *LOST AND BROKEN: MY JOURNEY BACK FROM CHRONIC PAIN AND CRIPPLING ANXIETY*

# FOSTER POSITIVITY

Replacing negative thoughts with positive thoughts is a true anxiety buster. The more you practice, the stronger that positivity muscle will develop.

Which areas of your life bring you down? Why? How do they impact you?

................................................................................................................

................................................................................................................

................................................................................................................

................................................................................................................

................................................................................................................

................................................................................................................

................................................................................................................

................................................................................................................

................................................................................................................

................................................................................................................

................................................................................................................

................................................................................................................

................................................................................................................

................................................................................................................

................................................................................................................

................................................................................................................

................................................................................................................

................................................................................................................

................................................................................................................

................................................................................................................

How can you view the negative areas in your life with fresh eyes? Practice reframing your negatives into positives.

Think of five situations that created painful anxiety, then identify the positive aspects or possible messages each may be communicating. What can you do to specifically address the problems or improve the situation?

# KEEP A GRATITUDE/ WINNING JOURNAL

Focusing far more on positive, uplifting thoughts counteracts a lapse into negative thoughts. Do you celebrate the good? What are you grateful to have in your life? At work? You can boost positivity by writing down three pleasant surprises you've had recently. What has felt like a win lately? Who could you share these wins with? If you don't like writing in a physical journal each night, apps like Day One, Gratitude Plus, and Flavors of Gratefulness may be your cup of tea.

Write down three things you feel particularly grateful for and why.

1 ............................................................................

............................................................................

2 ............................................................................

............................................................................

3 ............................................................................

............................................................................

"Man is not worried by real problems so much as by his imagined anxieties about real problems"

Epictetus

# RELAX IN NATURE

The hyperactivity of life can overstimulate your senses and leave you feeling detached from your own body. Disconnecting from modern life and reconnecting with nature can both ground and calm you. Connecting to the beauty around you can help you reconnect to your deepest, most tranquil self. Time spent in outdoor spaces has been shown to lower blood pressure and cortisol levels—stress hormones. Viewing green scenery engages the posterior cingulate cortex, which regulates stress responses. Create your own garden, go for a hike, visit your local park or garden.

List five places near you where you could go to specifically focus on and enjoy nature.

1

2

3

4

5

# BIRDSONG HAS A HEALING EFFECT

Two studies published in *Scientific Reports* revealed that seeing or hearing birds provides a significant positive benefit to mental health. If you can't spend a day around birds, listening to even six-minute audio clips of birdsong reduced feelings of anxiety, depression, and paranoia in study participants. The benefit was striking when compared to the deleterious effects of hearing traffic noise. If you feel anxious, spending ten minutes outside simply listening to the glorious sounds birds use to communicate may be just what the doctor ordered.

"Everybody needs beauty...places to play in and pray in where nature may heal and cheer and give strength to the body and soul alike."

John Muir

Now, let's discuss some more focused techniques for managing anxiety in your everyday life.

# USE MINDFULNESS MEDITATION TO CALM ANXIETY

Mindfulness is a focusing technique that encourages you to concentrate on feelings, thoughts, or bodily sensations happening within—*solely* in the present moment. This can help distract your brain from getting caught up in ruminative or other negative thought patterns. Mindfulness also helps you recognize the kinds of intrusive, nonproductive thoughts you need to consciously jettison, such as unrealistic fears.

Nonjudgmentally and compassionately focusing solely on what you're thinking or feeling in the present moment—then choosing to dismiss or alter unwelcome or distracting thoughts—helps you overcome anxiety. If practiced often enough, over time, mindfulness becomes ingrained.

Mindfulness also provides opportunities for us to gently observe something we typically resist seeing, thereby taking a fresh look at a familiar response. It's kind of like seeing the method to your madness.

# " THE HUMAN MIND IS LIKE A MOVIE THEATER THAT NEVER CLOSES—ALWAYS PREPARED TO SHOW FILMS OF WHAT WE FEAR. "

## —SUSAN M. ORSILLO AND LIZABETH ROEMER,

*THE MINDFUL WAY THROUGH ANXIETY*

# MINDFULNESS MEDITATIONS

All you need to practice mindfulness is five minutes and a quiet spot where you can sit undisturbed in a meditative state. As long as your feet are grounded on the floor, you can sit in a chair. Lay your hands on your lap, palms up or down, and, if you like, form a circle with your pointer finger and thumb. It's helpful to set a timer for five to ten minutes, and to make mindfulness meditation a habit. The more you practice, the sooner it will something you can automatically use when anxious.

Below and on the following pages are several mindfulness meditations to get you started. Once you've done these, come up with your own ideas. Remember, you don't have to be sitting on a cushion to access a meditative state. You can be mindful—pay attention to what's happening in the present—sitting, walking, cooking, dancing, or lying in bed.

## SOUND MEDITATION

Once you're settled comfortably in your meditating spot, close your eyes and focus on breathing slowly in and out for a few minutes. As thoughts arise, notice them then quickly dismiss them—envision butterflies flitting away—and refocus on your breath. Begin by simply listening to sounds around you. Without trying to identify them, just notice their timbre, volume, duration. You want to focus on the sensation of sound, bringing your attention back to those feelings or sensations every time it wanders.

Write about how it felt to focus solely on the sensations sounds create. How many did you notice? Did you have intrusive thoughts? Were you successful in dismissing them?

.......................................................................................................

.......................................................................................................

.......................................................................................................

.......................................................................................................

.......................................................................................................

.......................................................................................................

.......................................................................................................

## MUSIC MEDITATION

This time listen to a song you love. Shutting down all thought, focus on the instruments you can hear and the way each sound contributes to the whole. Write a paragraph about your experience. What music did you choose? Did you have to constantly jettison intrusive thoughts? How did it feel to listen closely to the unique sound of each instrument? How did this meditation feel in your body?

.......................................................................................................

.......................................................................................................

.......................................................................................................

.......................................................................................................

.......................................................................................................

.......................................................................................................

.......................................................................................................

.......................................................................................................

# SHOWERING OR BATHING MEDITATION

During this mindfulness meditation, keep your focus on the sensations you are experiencing: the temperature of the water, the sound of the shower, how it feels when the water strikes or envelopes your skin, how luxurious the soap feels when you apply it, how your body feels as you nurture it with bathing. The point is simply to be fully present in the moment, focusing your attention on the sensations of the experience and not allowing intrusive thoughts to interfere.

Write a paragraph about your experience. Were you able to dismiss intrusive thoughts and keep your focus solely on the physical sensations? What kept intruding? Did you enjoy the experience more than usual?

Try another version of this when you apply lotion to your body or put on your makeup or shave. All you have to do is focus solely on what's happening in the present moment, the movements you are making and the sensations you are feeling, all while keeping intrusive thoughts at bay. Write about the physical sensations and how focusing solely on bodily sensations impacted you. Did you find it relaxing? What other everyday activities offer opportunities for mindfulness?

"You are not your thoughts.
You are the observer of your thoughts."

Amit Ray, *Mindfulness: Living in the Moment,*
*Living in the Breath*

# HAPPY MEMORY MEDITATION

Once you are settled, focused on your breathing and calm, bring up a memory of an event that brought you great happiness. Try to see the memory as a movie taking place in your mind. Focus on re-experiencing the feelings, sounds, tastes, smells, colors, or whatever senses bolster the memory. Allow yourself to feel as if it's all happening again. Stick with this process, for ten minutes, bringing your focus back if it wanders.

How did it feel to recall such a happy memory? What brought it fully to life for you? What about this *particular* memory made it such a happy one?

Make a list of happy events in your life that you could call up when needed. Jot down details that will evoke the memory.

_____

_____

_____

_____

_____

_____

_____

_____

_____

_____

_____

_____

_____

_____

_____

_____

_____

_____

_____

_____

*Note: The next time you feel anxious, it's helpful to use this meditation to calm your mind.*

# MINDFULNESS IS INSTRUCTIVE

The more you practice paying attention to your thoughts as they occur in the present moment, the more you'll learn how your mind works. For example, you may find that your mind:

Is frequently hyperactive.

Often generates or amps up emotions.

Has fused with internal experiences.

Is often harsh and critical.

When practicing mindfulness, you want to solely notice and release thoughts, but writing about what those thoughts were later can help you identify trouble spots in how your mind processes.

*Note: Jon Kabat-Zinn hosts mindfulness meditations on his website (jonkabat-zinn.com).*

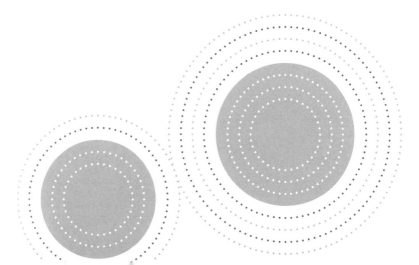

Mindfulness refers to the process of intentionally bringing your attention, in a nonjudgmental way, to the internal and external experiences occurring in the present moment. While encouraging openness, curiosity, and acceptance of your own process, this may include you being aware of sensations, thoughts, bodily states, consciousness, and the environment. Mindfulness is a skill that can be improved by practicing meditation on a regular basis.

The two core components of mindfulness are self-regulation of attention and orientation toward the present moment. Practicing mindfulness relieves stress caused by spending too much time focused on what happened in your past or what *might* happen in the future. This type of reflective observation also counters experiential avoidance—attempts to alter the intensity or frequency of undesirable or unwanted internal experiences.

The practice of mindfulness includes coming to recognize the faculty of awareness within and learning how to befriend and inhabit it as the primary dimension or abode of experience.

...............................................................................................................

"The richness of present moment experience is the richness of life itself. Too often we let our thinking and our beliefs about what we 'know' prevent us from seeing things as they really are."

...............................................................................................................

Jon Kabat-Zinn

# SAFE AND HAPPY MEDITATION

When anxious, it's helpful to spend five minutes mindfully envisioning a time in your life when you felt safe and happy. Once you've slowed your breathing and jettisoned any anxious thoughts, focus on re-envisioning a time in your life when you felt safe and happy. Focus on recalling specific details, particularly how you felt and what created that feeling. If you struggle to find a memory, create what would be an ideal situation and envision ideal details. The point is you can call up these memories when feeling anxious and immediately calm your anxiety.

Try visualizing a tranquil scene, such as a beach or meadow. See yourself frolicking in the sun. Feel the sun's warmth on your skin and the refreshment that comes with a cool breeze. Hear the sound of happy children, birds, or waves. Feel your toes in the water or your hands trailing through wildflowers.

How did it make you feel? Which details in your vision proved most meaningful?

What other scenarios would help you relax?

What details would help you re-experience or create the positive, happy feelings again? Engage each of your senses—sound, taste, sight, smell, touch.

" MEDITATION IS NOT A WAY OF MAKING YOUR MIND QUIET. IT'S A WAY OF ENTERING INTO THE QUIET THAT'S ALREADY THERE— BURIED UNDER THE 50,000 THOUGHTS THE AVERAGE PERSON THINKS EVERY DAY. "

—DEEPAK CHOPRA

# WALKING MEDITATION

Mindfully meditating while walking is easy. Simply bring yourself to a focused state of mindfulness, then slowly step forward with your left foot as you inhale. Feel each step fully as your foot touches the ground or floor. Walk as if your foot is kissing the Earth. Proceed to lift each leg and gently place your foot on the ground. When your mind wanders, refocus on one of your senses. Hear the sounds around you, notice how the air feels on your skin, relish how firmly your foot touches the ground, listen to the sounds of your body moving, feel your breath entering and exiting your belly or nose. Pause, breathe, and repeat. After you've taken about fifteen steps, pause to enjoy a cleansing and refocusing mindful breath. Turn around and walk the path again. Follow this practice for about five to ten minutes.

*Note: You can also mindfully walk by focusing solely on what you're seeing, hearing, smelling, touching, or feeling as you walk wherever you are.*

"I only went out for a walk, and finally concluded to stay out till sundown, for going out, I found, was really going in."

John Muir, *John of the Mountains: The Unpublished Journals of John Muir*

List five nearby areas where you could do a walking meditation and why each would make an ideal choice.

List three friends you could ask to join you on a walk.

Commit to making a walking date.

1
....................................................................................................................
....................................................................................................................
....................................................................................................................

2
....................................................................................................................
....................................................................................................................
....................................................................................................................

3
....................................................................................................................
....................................................................................................................
....................................................................................................................

....................................................................................................................

"You cannot be a gardener without mindfulness.
. . It's focused attention, a kind of single-pointed
meditation . . . the definition of mindfulness."
....................................................................................................................

Marc Hamer

According to Suze Yalof Schwartz, author of *Unplug: A Simple Guide to Meditation for Busy Skeptics and Modern Soul Seekers*, connecting with the Earth and the practice of gardening cultivates a mind that often feels calm and connected. Simply planting a seed with intention, or touching soil, can be mindfully transformative.

## HOW TO GARDEN MINDFULLY

Gather your materials for the task at hand. Take a long, slow deep breath. Notice nature around you, feel the soil, smell the air, welcome the sun.

Use a finger or your hand to create space, pause to notice how it feels to touch soil.

Hold the seeds or the plant in your hands and silently state your intentions for them to grow and be healthy. Gently place the seeds or plant into the ground, cover it with soil, and gently pat.

As you lightly water your new plant, listen to the sound of the water hitting the earth.

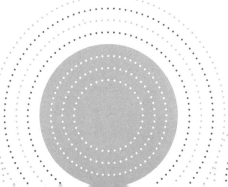

# PRACTICE YOGA TO ACHIEVE MULTIPLE BENEFITS

Another way to practice mindfulness is to learn yoga poses that will incorporate mindfulness and physical release.

Yoga is not simply a series of poses designed to stretch and strengthen muscles. It's a discipline designed to integrate body, mind, and spirit, which, when regularly practiced, can increase your energy while also calming your mind. Like muscle relaxation exercises in which you: tighten a group of muscles, focus your attention on them for a length of time breathing slowly in and out, then release and relax. Yoga helps reduce anxiety by redirecting your thoughts and bolstering deep breathing, focus, movement, release, and relaxation. Yoga is also a mindfulness practice.

Each of the following poses will help calm your nervous system and promote relaxation. The ones suggested are beginner level and should not cause any discomfort or pain to execute, but you still may want to attend a yoga class before performing. If you have any concerns, be sure to ask your doctor if it's safe for you to do these poses.

" YOGA IS THE DANCE OF EVERY CELL WITH THE MUSIC OF EVERY BREATH THAT CREATES INNER SERENITY AND HARMONY. "

—DR. DEBASISH MRIDHA

# TRY EASY POSE
# OR SUKHASANA

This simple sitting pose is designed to help you feel more grounded and less stressed out. Place a yoga mat or cushion on the floor and sit cross-legged on it. Place your hands around each knee with your palms facing upwards and each thumb and forefinger forming a circle. Straighten your spine and wiggle your bottom until your spine is perfectly aligned with your hips. As you inhale, imagine lifting your chest toward the sky, and, when you exhale, feel the release of breath grounding you through your hips. While breathing normally, hold this pose for three to five minutes. Release your legs and move to the next position.

"Inhale the future, exhale the past."

Anonymous

# UPWARD-FACING DOG OR URDHVA MUKHA SVANASANA

To stimulate your spinal cord and soothe your parasympathetic nervous system, lie face down on your yoga mat with your feet hip-width apart and the tops of your feet pressing against the mat. Place your hands beside your abdomen, palm down, with your fingers pointed toward the top of the mat. Inhale and push your upper torso up, lengthening your arms completely and pressing down through your palms.

Lift your torso upward and distribute your weight so your hands and your hips hold you in balance. Puff out your chest and rotate your shoulders back. With your upper back extended breathe for thirty seconds to one minute, then slowly lower your upper torso. To release, lift until you are resting your buttocks on your feet then move to a sitting position.

"Yoga has a sly, clever way of short circuiting the mental patterns that cause anxiety."

Baxter Bell

# FORWARD BEND OR UTTANASANA

To further lengthen and release tension in your spine, as well as stimulate your nervous system, bring your arms down your body while bending forward, from your hips—not your waist. Bring your hands to the mat, lining up your fingertips with your toes, then press your palms flat to the mat—or use blocks to shorten the distance—while keeping your knees straight, or softly bent but not locked. While holding the pose: with each inhalation, lift and lengthen your front torso just slightly, and, with each exhalation, release a little more fully into the forward bend. Hold until you're no longer comfortable. To come up, inhale and place your hands onto your hips. Press your tailbone down and contract your abdominal muscles as you slowly rise.

"The places where you have the most resistance [in yoga] are actually the places that are going to be the areas of the greatest liberation."

Rodney Yee

# CHILD'S POSE
# OR BALASANA

This pose simulates a mother holding her child, relaxing and breathing deeply in. It provides a sense of calm, comfort, contentment, and safety. Begin by kneeling on the floor, then bring your big toes together and sit on your heels. Separate your knees to align with your hips. Exhale and lean forward from your hips, positioning your torso between your thighs.

Move your hip bones outward to lengthen your tailbone and tuck your chin slightly to lift the base of your skull to stretch the back of your neck. You can either walk your hands toward the front of your mat or reach backwards toward your feet to rest your arms alongside your torso—palms up. Once in position, release your shoulders toward the floor. Since this is a resting pose, you should be comfortable holding it for five minutes or so while breathing normally.

To come up: first lengthen your front torso, then, with an inhalation, lift from your tailbone as it presses down and into the pelvis.

# CORPSE POSE OR SAVASANA

This is the resting pose typically done at the end of a yoga session. It's designed to release all tension, clear your mind, and refresh your body. For this pose, lie down on your back then straighten and separate your legs. Place your arms alongside your body, slightly separated from your torso, with palms upwards but relaxed, allowing your fingers to curl in. Tuck your shoulder blades in for more back support.

Once you're in position, relax your whole body—including your face. Lie still and breathe naturally while keeping your mind free of thoughts. Some people like listening to gentle music and setting a timer to help with focus, but simply noticing your breath and the quiet is also relaxing. Work toward staying in this pose for ten minutes.

To come out, while keeping your eyes closed, slowly deepen your breath, wiggle your fingers and toes, then gradually raise your arms overhead and stretch upwards from your hands and downward from your feet. Bring your knees to your chest, roll over to one side, then use your bottom arm as a pillow and pause for a moment curled into a fetal position. After a few breaths, use your hands to lift you back to a sitting position.

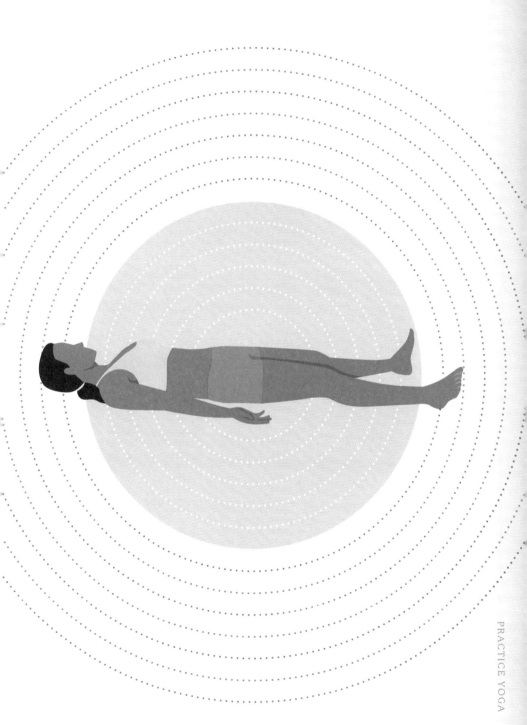

# GET IN SYNC WITH OTHERS

In *Synchrony and Cooperation*, authors Scott Wiltermuth and Chip Heath suggest that acting in synchrony with others—be it while walking, singing, or dancing—can increase cooperation and collectivism among group members. "In a yoga class, everyone is moving and breathing in at the same time, [which is] one of the undervalued mechanisms that yoga can really help with: giving people that sense of belonging, of being part of something bigger."

We've given you an arsenal of techniques to address, subvert, and overcome anxiety. As a final reminder, we'll now discuss well-known essentials.

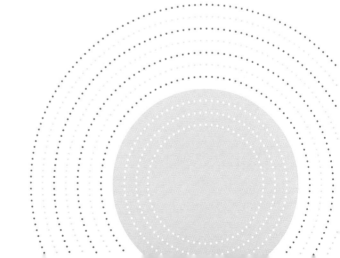

66

THE NATURE
OF YOGA IS TO
SHINE THE LIGHT OF
AWARENESS INTO THE
DARKEST CORNERS
OF THE BODY.

99

—JASON CRANDELL

# BOOST YOUR OVERALL HEALTH

Obviously eating a healthy diet, sleeping well at night, and exercising are all beneficial to your ability to overcome anxiety, so let's discuss some essential reminders.

## EAT WELL

Eating a healthy, well-balanced diet is beneficial to your body and brain. The more you choose fresh, nutrient-rich food and avoid or limit saturated fats, high carbs, sugar, processed foods, alcohol, and caffeine, the more smoothly your body and brain will function. Either the Mediterranean or MIND (Mediterranean Intervention for Neurodegenerative Delay) diet offer highly recommended parameters.

Food that helps your body combat anxiety include:

Potassium-rich foods such as pumpkin seeds or bananas

Zinc-rich foods such as walnuts, pecans, and almonds

Foods rich in vitamin B such as beef, pork, chicken, leafy greens, legumes, citrus fruits, rice, nuts, and eggs

Tryptophan-containing foods such as turkey, eggs, dark chocolate, cheese, pineapple, bananas, oats, and tofu

Chia seeds, which are a good source of omega-3s.

If you don't know what changes you need to make or have any diet concerns, please discuss your current diet with your doctor. Meanwhile, let's identify any problem areas.

What do your meals look like over a week?

What are your eating pitfalls?

Which specific foods or habits do you need to jettison?

Which specific foods do you need to add?

................................................................................................................

................................................................................................................

................................................................................................................

................................................................................................................

................................................................................................................

................................................................................................................

................................................................................................................

................................................................................................................

................................................................................................................

................................................................................................................

................................................................................................................

................................................................................................................

................................................................................................................

................................................................................................................

................................................................................................................

................................................................................................................

................................................................................................................

................................................................................................................

................................................................................................................

................................................................................................................

................................................................................................................

................................................................................................................

................................................................................................................

................................................................................................................

................................................................................................................

How can you improve your daily eating habits?

.......................................................................................................................................................
.......................................................................................................................................................
.......................................................................................................................................................
.......................................................................................................................................................
.......................................................................................................................................................
.......................................................................................................................................................
.......................................................................................................................................................
.......................................................................................................................................................
.......................................................................................................................................................
.......................................................................................................................................................
.......................................................................................................................................................
.......................................................................................................................................................
.......................................................................................................................................................
.......................................................................................................................................................
.......................................................................................................................................................
.......................................................................................................................................................
.......................................................................................................................................................
.......................................................................................................................................................
.......................................................................................................................................................
.......................................................................................................................................................
.......................................................................................................................................................

# SLEEP WELL

Quality sleep matters! As you sleep, your brain refreshes itself. Putting down cell phones, computers, or video games at least an hour before bed; taking a warm bath or shower; reading something relaxing; and transitioning into quiet and darkness will all ease you into sleep. It's also helpful to write down what you need to do the next day and anything that is troubling you. It's also helpful to do a mindfulness meditation focused on relaxing each muscle group in your body while releasing all thoughts. Once you're sound asleep, your brain will shift into REM sleep, where it sorts your troubling thoughts and often comes up with solutions.

According to the Center for Disease Control and Prevention, to develop habits that can improve your sleep health you should:

- Be consistent—go to bed at the same time each night and get up at the same time each morning, including weekends

- Make sure your bedroom is quiet, dark, relaxing, and at a comfortable temperature

- Remove electronic devices—such as TVs, computers, and smart phones—from the bedroom

- Avoid large meals, caffeine, and alcohol before bedtime

- Exercise regularly—being physically active during the day can help you fall asleep more easily at night.

For adults, a minimum of seven hours of sleep per night is recommended. If you have consistent problems sleeping, talk with your doctor.

What are your sleep habits? Do they need adjustment? What can you do to improve your sleeping environment?

List five habits you can adopt to relax before bed.

1

2

3

4

5

"If you want to conquer the anxiety of life,
live in the moment, live in the breath."

Amit Ray

# MOVE YOUR BODY REGULARLY

One of the many benefits of regular exercise is that it reduces stress and helps you sleep well at night. In fact, vigorously moving your body on a regular basis has a multitude of benefits—beyond distraction—for overcoming anxiety. These include:

It boosts serotonin, reducing depression and increasing subjective feelings of well-being

It metabolizes the panic chemicals—adrenaline and thyroxin—and relieves pent-up frustration

It helps stabilize your mental state, reducing use of drugs and alcohol

It enhances oxygenation of blood flowing to your brain, bolstering concentration and memory

It stimulates endorphins, increasing happiness and self-esteem

It improves sleep.

For exercise to have the most benefit it should be aerobic—increase your heart rate for ten minutes—and take place four to five times a week for twenty to thirty minutes at a time. Dancing, jogging, swimming, cycling, or brisk walking are all good options.

Do you get regular, strenuous exercise? List three forms of vigorous activities you could adopt on a regular basis.

1 .......................................................................................................

.......................................................................................................

2 .......................................................................................................

.......................................................................................................

3 .......................................................................................................

.......................................................................................................

Identify your resistance to exercise, then list three ways you can ramp it up. What would help you get in the habit of being physically active?

1 .......................................................................................................

.......................................................................................................

2 .......................................................................................................

.......................................................................................................

3 .......................................................................................................

.......................................................................................................

# GET STARTED AND STAY MOTIVATED

The Mayo Clinic recommends becoming physically active on a regular basis include by doing some of the following:

Identify what you enjoy doing—the type of physical activities you're most likely to do—and pinpoint when and how you'd be most likely to follow through.

Discuss an exercise program or physical activity routine and how it fits into your overall treatment plan with your doctor.

Set reasonable goals. Tailor your plan to your own needs and abilities rather than setting unrealistic guidelines that you're unlikely to meet.

Don't think of exercise or physical activity as a chore. If it's just another "should" in your life that you aren't living up to, you'll associate it with failure. View it as therapy—a tool to help you get better.

Analyze your barriers. Figure out what's stopping you from being physically active or exercising. Find an alternative solution.

Prepare for setbacks and obstacles. Give yourself credit for every step in the right direction, no matter how small. If you skip it one day, try again the next day. Stick with it.

"

TYPICALLY,
PEOPLE
WHO EXERCISE
START EATING BETTER
AND BECOMING MORE
PRODUCTIVE AT WORK. THEY
SMOKE LESS AND SHOW
MORE PATIENCE WITH
COLLEAGUES AND
FAMILY.

THEY
USE THEIR
CREDIT CARDS LESS
FREQUENTLY AND SAY
THEY FEEL LESS STRESSED...
EXERCISE IS A KEYSTONE
HABIT THAT TRIGGERS
WIDESPREAD
CHANGE.

"

—CHARLES DUHIGG,
*THE POWER OF HABIT: WHY WE DO*
*WHAT WE DO IN LIFE AND BUSINESS*

# BOOST YOUR MOOD
# BY WALKING

In a 2007 study by Bowling Green University, thirty-six participants kept mood diaries during the first and final four weeks of a sixteen-week weight loss program. Participants who engaged in planned exercise—typically walking for thirty to sixty minutes a day—reported a better mood at night as compared to in the morning, before exercising.

Walking in nature, versus an urban environment, has been shown to decrease self-rumination; which is often linked to depression and other mental illnesses.

What are three ways you can boost the number of steps you take each day?

1

2

3

"...JUST BE, WHATEVER YOU ARE WITH WHATEVER YOU HAVE, AND REALIZE THAT THAT IS ENOUGH TO BE HAPPY. THERE'S A WHOLE WORLD OUT THERE, RIGHT OUTSIDE YOUR WINDOW. YOU'D BE A FOOL TO MISS IT."

—CHARLOTTE ERIKSSON

# GIVE TAI CHI A CHANCE

Practicing tai chi can provide the same benefits for managing stress-related anxiety as exercise. The slow, mindful breaths and movements have a positive effect on the nervous system and mood-regulating hormones which may make tai chi superior to other forms of exercise for reducing stress and anxiety.

"Your quality of experience is based not on standards such as time or ranking, but on finally awakening to an awareness of the fluidity within action itself."

Haruki Murakami, *What I Talk About When I Talk About Running*

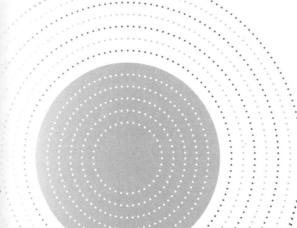

## WE'VE COME TO THE END OF OUR JOURNEY TOWARD MASTERING ANXIETY.

If you use the techniques you've learned, you should begin to see anxiety become manageable and a renewed vigor kick your life into high gear. Remember to reinforce the techniques you've learned and promptly address anxiety when it arises.

........................................................

"Yesterday I was clever, so I wanted to change the world. Today I am wise, so I am changing myself."

........................................................

Rumi

"I hope to one day see a sea of
people all wearing silver ribbons
as a sign that they understand the
secret battle [with anxiety], and as
a celebration of the victories made
each day as we individually pull
ourselves up out of our foxholes to
see our scars heal, and to remember
what the sun looks like."

Jenny Lawson, *Furiously Happy: A Funny Book About
Horrible Things*

# ABOUT THE AUTHOR

Susan Reynolds has written, co-authored, or edited more than 25 nonfiction books, primarily self-help works on everything from finance to meditation to neuroscience. Her books include *5-Minute Productivity Workbook*, *3-Minute Positivity Workbook*, *Fire Up Your Writing Brain*, and *Train Your Brain to Get Happy*. She regularly blogs for Psychologytoday.com and on fireupyourwritingbrain.com.

# REFERENCES

American Psychiatric Association. (2013). Diagnostic and statistical manual of mental disorders (5th ed.).

Berger, B. G., Darby, L. A., Owen, D. R., & Carels, R. A. (2023). "Feeling good" after exercise during a weight loss program: subjective well-being in support of a hedonic paradigm. *Perceptual and Motor Skills, 130*(1), 434-460. https://doi.org/10.1177/00315125221130444

Borne, E. J. & Garano, L. (2016) Copying with anxiety: 10 simple ways to relieve anxiety, fear, and worry. New Harbinger.

Carbonell, D. & Auldridge, S.P, Jr, *et al.* (2016). The worry trick: how your brain tricks you into expecting the worst and what you can do about it. New Harbinger.

Fisher, J.C., Dallimer, M., Irvine, K.N. et al. Human well-being responses to species' traits. *Nat Sustain* (2023). https://doi.org/10.1038/s41893-023-01151-3

Laskowski ER (expert opinion). Mayo Clinic. June 16, 2021

McDonald, M. C. (2023) Unbroken: the trauma response is never wrong: and other things you need to know to take back your life. Sounds True.

National Center for Chronic Disease Prevention and Health Promotion, Division of Population Health (2022). How Much Sleep Do I Need? https://www.cdc.gov/sleep/about_sleep/how_much_sleep

O'Connor, Peg. (2017) *Anxiety is part of human nature.* Psychology Today, https://www.psychologytoday.com/us/blog/philosophy-stirred-not-shaken/201703/anxiety-is-part-human-nature

Orsillo, S. M., & Roemer, L. (2011). The mindful way through anxiety: Break free from chronic worry and reclaim your life. The Guilford Press.

Scher, A. (2019). How to heal yourself from anxiety when no one else can. Llewelyn.

Schwartz, S. Y. (2017) Unplug: a simple guide to mediation for skeptics and modern soul seekers. Harmony.

Wiltermuth, S. S., & Heath, C. (2009). Synchrony and cooperation. *Psychological Science, 20*(1), 1-5. https://doi.org/10.1111/j.1467-9280.2008.02253.x